Contents

GN00983490

Amazing Grace
978-0-9570793-6-6

Nihil Obstat: Father Anton Cowan, Censor
Imprimatur: The Most Reverend Vincent Nichols, Archbishop of Westminster
Date: Ash Wednesday - 13 February 2013

The Nihil obstat *and* Imprimatur *are a declaration that a book or pamphlet is considered to be free from doctrinal or moral error. It is not implied that those who have granted the* Nihil obstat *and* Imprimatur *agree with the contents, opinions or statements expressed.*

Written by: Dr Mark Nash and Mrs Margaret Wickware
With thanks to Fr Gerard Sheehan and Fr Michael O'Boy for their comments and suggestions.

The Diocese of Westminster's Agency for Evangelisation is grateful to the National Council of the Churches of Christ in the U.S.A for use of the New Revised Standard Version Bible: Catholic Edition copyright © 1993 and 1989. Excerpts from The Divine Office © 1974, hierarchies of Australia, England and Wales, Ireland. All rights reserved.

All of the images contained in this booklet have been taken from those freely available at the Wikimedia Commons website and diocesan stock.

Produced by Agency for Evangelisation, Vaughan House, 46 Francis Street, London, SW1P 1QN. Tel: 020 7798 9152; email: evangelisation@rcdow.org.uk

 booklets are published by WRCDT. Design by Mark Nash.
Print arranged by Transform Management Ltd
info@1025transform.co.uk

The Diocese of Westminster's Agency for Evangelisation is committed to a sustainable future for our planet. The booklet in your hands is made from paper certified by the Forest Stewardship Council.

# Foreword

Dear Brothers and Sisters,

This Year of Faith, which started last 11 October and continues until 24 November 2013, presents us with many opportunities to reflect on the gift of faith and our personal call to holiness. So too does it offer us the time to contemplate afresh our relationship with the heavenly Father and encourages us towards a celebration of our faith with greater depth and gratitude.

In announcing the Year of Faith, the Holy Father wrote of using this year to retrace the history of our faith 'marked as it is by the unfathomable mystery of the interweaving of holiness and sin.' Such a retracing, through Scripture, through the life of the Church and her children, serves to highlight Christian witness and the need for each member of Christ's body to continue 'the work of conversion in order to experience the mercy of the Father which is held out to everyone' (*Porta Fidei*, 3).

Sparks of Light, a previous faith-sharing resource, encouraged groups and individuals to explore the call to holiness through the lives of the saints. *Amazing Grace*, which I commend to you this Lent, looks afresh as this 'continuing work of conversion', the desire for forgiveness and the inexhaustible mercy of our loving Father.

Throughout this season of sharing let us aspire to St Paul's vision of the believing community, as we read in his words to the community at Colossae: 'Bear with one another and, if anyone has a complaint against another, forgive each other; just as the Lord has forgiven you, so you also must forgive. Above all, clothe yourselves with love, which binds everything together in perfect harmony. Let the peace of Christ rule in your hearts… Let the word of Christ dwell in you richly' (Colossians 3:12-17).

Yours devotedly,

+ Vincent Nichols

The Most Reverend Vincent Nichols
Archbishop of Westminster

About this book

'It is not easy for man, wounded by sin, to maintain moral balance. Christ's gift of salvation offers us the grace necessary to persevere in the pursuit of the virtues. Everyone should always ask for this grace of light and strength, frequent the sacraments, cooperate with the Holy Spirit, and follow the Spirit's calls to love what is good and shun evil' (Catechism of the Catholic Church, 1811).

The reality of sin co-exists with the reality of holiness in our broken world. As Christians we are called to practice the virtues and aspire to holiness but the Church recognises our frequent failure to live up to the ideal. In the sacraments we have opportunities to reaquaint ourselves with God's love and his Son's redemptive act.

Amazing Grace is divided into six group sessions. Sessions One to Three retrace the relationship of God and humankind through the Scriptures in terms of the ebb and flow of holiness and sin. Sessions Four, Five and Six look at the reality of temptation, the call to continuing conversion and the healing power of the sacraments, specifically the Sacrament of Reconciliation.

In addition to the Scripture and reflections now familiar to users of *exploring faith* booklets, you will find a short description of the Sacraments in the context of reconciliation and a sprinkling of 'definitions' of terms found in the booklet. The Scripture passages have been chosen to reflect the theme of their respective sessions but you will benefit from reading the passage in context (that is, reading the passages before and after the one chosen) either as a group or individually.

The group sessions are illustrated with a selection of pictures on the purple backed pages and looking upon these images may stir a thought or feeling in a way that the text could not. We also invite you to make use of the daily prayers in the second part of the booklet which are drawn from the Divine Office.

Amazing Grace is not tied to a particular time of year and the prayers and meditations may be used by individuals, groups or in a wider parish context throughout the year. Additional reflections and thoughts can be found on our small group blog - *a threefold cord is not easily broken* [http://dowsmallgroups. wordpress.com]. This booklet and others in the *exploring faith* series can be viewed at and downloaded from http://issuu.com/exploringfaith/docs/.

The Garden of Earthly Delights by Hieronymus Bosch (1480-1505)

Reconciled by the Sacraments

Commemorating both the fiftieth anniversary of the opening of the Second Vatican Council and the twentieth anniversary of the publication of the Catechism of the Catholic Church, Pope Benedict XVI opened the Year of Faith with a call to rediscover the content of the faith that is professed, celebrated, lived and prayed.

Through the use of perceptible signs, words and actions, the Church celebrates the essence of our faith - the paschal mystery (CCC, 1084,1067). For centuries God planned our salvation and it came to pass: Christ died for our sins in accordance with the Scriptures, he was buried and he was raised on the third day (1 Corinthians 15:3-5). In doing so; God reconciled all of humankind to himself through his beloved Son. While Christ lived over 2000 years ago, his passion, death, resurrection and ascension are celebrated - made present in the sacramental life of the Church. Through these liturgical celebrations, we are invited to enter into this mystery of our faith - to join ourselves with Christ - to be reconciled.

A particular sacramental celebration may have happened many years ago or just yesterday yet God's work of reconciliation is on-going. Through the gift of his graces - blessings poured out on each of us and the continuous workings of the Holy Spirit - willing hearts are opened and transformed so that we may enter ever more deeply into the mystery.

The Washing of the Disciples' Feet by Francis Hoyland
John 13:1-17

Why did God put us here? **Amazing Grac**

Why did God put us here?

Opening Prayers

Taken from Psalm 103 (102) - to be said all together or the group can divide in half and alternate

All: In the name of the Father, and of the Son, and of the Holy Spirit. Amen.

A: My soul, give thanks to the Lord
all my being, bless his holy name.
My soul, give thanks to the Lord
and never forget all his blessings.

B: It is he who forgives all your guilt,
who heals every one of your ills,
who redeems your life from the grave,
who crowns you with love and compassion.

A: The Lord is compassion and love,
slow to anger and rich in mercy.
His wrath will come to an end;
he will not be angry for ever.
He does not treat us according to our sins
nor repay us according to our faults.

B: For as the heavens are high above the earth
so strong is his love for those who fear him.
As far as the east is from the west
so far does he remove our sins.

A: The love of the Lord is everlasting
upon those who hold him in fear;
his justice reaches out to children's children
when they keep his covenant in truth,
when they keep his will in their mind.

All: Glory be to the Father, and to the Son and to the Holy Spirit. As it was in the beginning, is now, and ever shall be, world without end. Amen.

As we come together let us, either aloud or in the silence of our hearts, give thanks and praise to the Lord for all the things we have accomplished, the joys experienced, graces received and people met over the past week. Let us also remember all those in need of our prayers.

Introduction to the Scripture reading
Let us listen carefully to the Word of the Lord,
and attend to it with the ear of our hearts.
Let us welcome it, and faithfully put it into practice.

St. Benedict of Nursia (c.480-c.547) adapted

Explore the Scriptures Romans 8:31-39
What then are we to say about these things? If God is for us, who is against us? He who did not withhold his own Son, but gave him up for all of us, will he not with him also give us everything else? Who will bring any charge against God's elect? It is God who justifies. Who is to condemn? It is Christ Jesus, who died, yes, who was raised, who is at the right hand of God, who indeed intercedes for us. Who will separate us from the love of Christ? Will hardship, or distress, or persecution, or famine, or nakedness, or peril, or sword? As it is written,

'For your sake we are being killed all day long;
    we are accounted as sheep to be slaughtered.'

No, in all these things we are more than conquerors through him who loved us. For I am convinced that neither death, nor life, nor angels, nor rulers, nor things present, nor things to come, nor powers, nor height, nor depth, nor anything else in all creation, will be able to separate us from the love of God in Christ Jesus our Lord.

Please take a few moments in silence to reflect on the passage, then share a word or phrase that has struck you. Pause to think about what others have said then, after a second reading of the passage, you may wish to share a further thought.

Reflection
Questions that even vaguely point to the biblical accounts of creation can often cause many of us to fall silent, unsure of how best to explain the Church's teaching and generally uncomfortable with the prospects of where the conversation might be heading. Week upon week, however, we begin our profession of faith with the words 'I believe in God, the Father Almighty, Creator of heaven and earth, all things visible and invisible.' yet our response to those who the popular press have armed with bits of information is often a deafening silence.

At the outset, the above question may seem rather daunting. Yet, aided by the *Catechism of the Catholic Church* and the writings of Pope Benedict XVI and his

Why did God put us here? **Amazing Grace**

predecessor, the late Blessed John Paul II, we have been guided to a fuller, deeper understanding of the symbolic narrative set out in the first pages of the Book of Genesis. While the *Catechism* reminds us that the Old Testament prefigures the work of Christ (CCC 128), Pope Benedict XVI (in a compilation of homilies entitled *In the Beginning*) explains that even from the beginning of time, Christ's message was being made known to us. Just as Christ so loved each one of us that he gave up his life, 'God created the universe in order to enter into a history of love with humankind. He created it so that love could exist'.

God did not create the universe for his own glory, nor was it simply by chance. It was his will to 'make creatures share in his being' (CCC 295). Thus, together, the Father, Son and Holy Spirit created humankind 'in their own image'. 'God shaped man from the soil of the ground and blew the breath of life into his nostrils, and man became a living being'. (Genesis 2:7). In doing so, our loving God wanted to be united as one with each of us, not just in a superficial way but as vital part of our very beings.

By giving the breath of life, God wished to live in an intimate relationship not just with Adam and Eve but also with every human being. Moreover, by his eternal plan, 'a bond still more intimate than that of creation' would be forthcoming. Through the pure gift of the Son himself, we would be offered participation in the very life of the Trinity. (*Dives in Misericordia*, 7).

While we were 'called into existence through love', Blessed John Paul II makes clear that at the same time we were 'called for love', to seek the good (*Familiaris Consortio*, 11). Our vocation, that is our fundamental mission, is to love, to seek an intimate relationship with Jesus Christ, to live by faith.

The Creation of Adam by Michelangelo (c.1511)

How would you characterise your relationship to God? How would you describe God to others? Does the way you talk about God to others depend on your relationship with them?

Closing Prayers
You may wish to end this session with some different prayers, the Our Father or silent reflection.

Almighty God,
you are the Father of us all.
You created the human family
to dwell for ever with you
and to praise your glory.
Open our ears to hear your voice
so that we might return to you
with sincere repentance for our sins.
Teach us to see in you our loving Father,
full of compassion for all who call to you for help.
Through Christ our Lord.
Amen.

Notes

What is meant by a 'virtue'? A virtue is an interior disposition, a positive habit, a passion that has been placed at the service of the good (*YOUCAT, 299)

* YOUCAT is the Youth Catechism of the Catholic Church

Signpost

This session looked at the how God created the world out of love, not for his glory but to share his being. Simply put we are invited to share in God's love. The next session will look at the ebb and low of the relationship between God and his chosen people - a relationship which pointed towards the coming of the Christ.

Why did God put us here? Amazing Grac

Building of the Tower of Babel from the 'Bedford Hours' by the Bedford Master (c.1410-1430)

Reconciled by the Sacraments - Holy Matrimony

At the very heart of the sacrament of holy matrimony and the married state lies the idea of self-giving – living for another, reconciling oneself to life for another, loving and being loved back in great measure. While frequently writing of the married vocation, Blessed Pope John Paul II gifted to the Church the great legacy of the Theology of the Body. Rooted in the Creation Story, Theology of the Body traces the path of our relationship with God, abandoned by Adam and Eve in their decision to sin. On our behalf, however, Christ endured intense physical pain from scourging and ultimately gave up his body for us so that we could be reconciled to the Lord. Through this redemptive work, he reveals the nature of true love and restored the original meaning of marriage.

'It is therefore fitting that spouses should seal their consent to give themselves to each other through the offering of their own lives by uniting it to the offering of Christ for his Church made present in the Eucharist sacrifice, and by receiving the Eucharist, communicating in the same Body and the same Blood of Christ, they may form "one body" in Christ' (CCC, 1621).

The Marriage at Cana by Francis Hoyland
John 2:1-11

Definitions - What is Grace?

By grace we mean God's free, loving gift to us, his helping goodness, the vitality that comes from him. Through the Cross and Resurrection, God devotes himself entirely to us and communicates himself to us in grace. Grace is everything God grants us, without our deserving it in the least (YOUCAT, 338).

* YOUCAT is the Youth Catechism of the Catholic Church

Risings and fallings

Opening Prayers

Taken from Psalm 4 - to be said all together or the group can divide in half and alternate

All: In the name of the Father, and of the Son, and of the Holy Spirit. Amen.

A: When I call, answer me, O God of justice;
from anguish you released me, have mercy and hear me!

B: O men, how long will your hearts be closed,
will you love what is futile and seek what is false?

A: It is the Lord who grants favours to those whom he loves;
the Lord hears me whenever I call him.

B: Fear him; do not sin: ponder on your bed and be still
Make justice your sacrifice, and trust in the Lord.

A: 'What can bring us happiness?' many say.
Lift up the light of your face on us, O Lord.

B: You have put into my heart a greater joy
than they have from abundance of corn and new wine.

A: I will lie down in peace and sleep comes at once
for you alone, Lord, make me dwell in safety.

All: Glory be to the Father, and to the Son and to the Holy Spirit. As it was in
the beginning, is now, and ever shall be, world without end. Amen.

*As we come together let us, either aloud or in the silence of our hearts, give thanks
and praise to the Lord for all the things we have accomplished, the joys experienced,
graces received and people met over the past week. Let us also remember all those in
need of our prayers.*

Introduction to the Scripture reading
Let us listen carefully to the Word of the Lord,
and attend to it with the ear of our hearts.
Let us welcome it, and faithfully put it into practice.

St. Benedict of Nursia (c.480-c.547) adapted

Explore the Scriptures Ezekiel 36:22-30

Therefore say to the house of Israel, Thus says the Lord God: It is not for your sake, O house of Israel, that I am about to act, but for the sake of my holy name, which you have profaned among the nations to which you came. I will sanctify my great name, which has been profaned among the nations, and which you have profaned among them; and the nations shall know that I am the Lord, says the Lord God, when through you I display my holiness before their eyes. I will take you from the nations, and gather you from all the countries, and bring you into your own land. I will sprinkle clean water upon you, and you shall be clean from all your uncleannesses, and from all your idols I will cleanse you.

A new heart I will give you, and a new spirit I will put within you; and I will remove from your body the heart of stone and give you a heart of flesh. I will put my spirit within you, and make you follow my statutes and be careful to observe my ordinances. Then you shall live in the land that I gave to your ancestors; and you shall be my people, and I will be your God. I will save you from all your uncleannesses, and I will summon the grain and make it abundant and lay no famine upon you. I will make the fruit of the tree and the produce of the field abundant, so that you may never again suffer the disgrace of famine among the nations.

Please take a few moments in silence to reflect on the passage, then share a word or phrase that has struck you. Pause to think about what others have said then, after a second reading of the passage, you may wish to share a further thought.

Reflection

Whether we live in a large cosmopolitan city or a tiny hamlet, life in the 21st century is so dramatically different from Old Testament times that it can sometimes be difficult to see its relevance to our daily lives. Yet we believe that Christ's Incarnation was not by chance, a spur of the moment decision. On the contrary, over the preceding centuries, God had gradually gathered a people to himself to prepare them for his greatest gift, his Son. As with any relationship at times it was, and is, severely tested and it is only by the deep love of one for the other that it prevails.

Adam and Eve freely chose to reject God's invitation to live in his loving embrace, yet he did not simply cast them aside. He blessed our first parents with children and made an enduring promise - a covenant that he would stamp out the evil that had won their attention in the Garden of Eden (Genesis 3:1-24). Although our just God made their lives more difficult, his love did not falter.

Continuing through the pages of Scripture, we read that their descendants again and again chose to turn away from God, to sin. Yet, he was undeterred and he renewed his promise to humanity through a good and upright man, Noah and later Abraham, our father in faith. God was always willing to give a fresh start. In time, God's chosen people came to know his love and compassion when they were freed from slavery in Egypt and they sang in his honour: 'The Lord is my strength and my song, to him I owe my deliverance, He is my God and I shall praise him' (Exodus 15:2). Sadly, however, their initial willingness to live by the commandments given to Moses was quickly forgotten but yet again, despite this, the Lord promised his steadfast love to his chosen people (Exodus 24:3, 34:10).

In all of this we see God's mercy at work. Mercy, so often misunderstood as pity, is the all-embracing love, 'noticed particularly in suffering, injustice and poverty' that call us back to him despite our many limitations and frailties, our sins and infidelities (*Dives in Misericordia*, 3 and 4). While King David's cry for mercy is perhaps most well known (Psalm 5:2), throughout the Old Testament, the prophets: Hosea, Micah and Jeremiah among others frequently called upon the Israelites to seek God's mercy and forgiveness for their infidelities – when material goods, pleasure and personal needs took precedence over the Lord. While it seemed that God's relationship with his people had all but dissolved, his inextinguishable compassion persisted and small groups of faithful Jews (the Maccabeans, the Pharasees, Sadduces and Essence, among others) continued to practice the Law and to seek his mercy. Yet, the prophet Ezekiel (36:22-32) challenged the Israelites - 'what right do we have to seek God's compassion and mercy?' He announced that the covenant was not only communal but also personal, to be written on the hearts of his chosen people and to be the standard for daily living, their way of life.

The L to R: Hosea, Jeremiah and Ezekiel by Duccio di Buoninsegna (1308-1311)

In face of traumatic circumstances, (the Destruction of the Temple, exile from their Promised Land and rule by the Babylonians), the latter prophets stirred the hearts of the Israelites, encouraging them to live righteously – in harmony with God. Together, they prayed for the coming of the promised Messiah. Together, they waited in hope for the descendant of David, Immanuel, to be born in Bethlehem.

Does the slow evolution of Israel's faith in any way mirror our own journey of faith? How do you react to the call of the prophetic voices in your life? Are you a prophet?

Closing Prayers
You may wish to end this session with some different prayers, the Our Father or silent reflection.

God our Father,
you chose us to be your children,
to be holy in your sight
and happy in your presence.
Receive us as a loving Father
so that we may share the joy and love of your holy Church.
Through Christ our Lord.
Amen.

 Notes

Signpost

This session looked through the books of Sacred Scripture at the many failings that God's chosen people experienced. God's hand was extended in mercy and the prophets continued to provide the message of repentance and love. Next session looks at the promised Messiah, the one who was to make all things right.

Flight into Egypt by Julius Schnorr von Carolsfeld (1828)

Reconciled by the Sacraments - Holy Orders

In reading through the Old Testament, we learn of priests, prophets and kings who led God's chosen people. From the time of Moses, ordained priests not only taught the Law of the Lord but also offered sacrifices on behalf of individuals and the community. These offerings, oftentimes a prized animal, were offered as gifts to God in hopes of healing or strengthening a relationship - either with God himself or another member of the community. The ritual associated with the sacrifice was not the source of forgiveness but an opportunity for God to communicate his mercy (Leviticus 4:20).

During his ministry, Christ himself forgave those with faith: the blind man, the paralytic and the adulteress, to mention but a few. Most importantly, he empowered the apostles and their successors to forgive sins. Having breathed on them, the apostles received a special outpouring of the Holy Spirit (Acts 1:80).

In similar fashion today, the anointing that takes place in the sacrament of holy orders 'configures the recipient to Christ by a special grace of the Holy Spirit' (CCC 1581). In doing so, the gift of gratuitous grace that reconciles all baptised to the Father is made particular. By his ordination, the priest is entrusted with the power to forgive sins in Christ's name. 'The priest is the sign and instrument of God's merciful love for the sinner' (CCC 1441, 1465).

The Choosing of the Twelve by Francis Hoyland
Matthew 10:2-4; Mark 3:13-19; Luke 6:12-19

What shall we do? **Amazing Grac**

What shall we do?

Opening Prayers

Taken from Psalm 105 (104) - to be said all together or the group can divide in half and alternate

All: In the name of the Father, and of the Son, and of the Holy Spirit. Amen.

A: Give thanks to the Lord, tell his name,
make known his deeds among the peoples.
O sing to him, sing his praise;
tell all his wonderful works!

B: Be proud of his holy name,
let the hearts that seek the Lord rejoice.
Consider the Lord and his strength.;
constantly seek his face.

A: O children of Abraham, his servant,
O sons of the Jacob he chose.
He, the Lord, is our God:
his judgements prevail in all the earth.

B: He remembers his covenant for ever,
his promise for a thousand generations,
the covenant he made with Abraham,
the oath he swore to Isaac.

All: Glory be to the Father, and to the Son and to the Holy Spirit. As it was in the beginning, is now, and ever shall be, world without end. Amen.

As we come together let us, either aloud or in the silence of our hearts, give thanks and praise to the Lord for all the things we have accomplished, the joys experienced, graces received and people met over the past week. Let us also remember all those in need of our prayers.

Introduction to the Scripture reading

Let us listen carefully to the Word of the Lord,
and attend to it with the ear of our hearts.
Let us welcome it, and faithfully put it into practice.

St. Benedict of Nursia (c.480-c.547) adapted

Explore the Scriptures Romans 6:1-11, 17-18, 23

What then are we to say? Should we continue in sin in order that grace may abound? By no means! How can we who died to sin go on living in it? Do you not know that all of us who have been baptised into Christ Jesus were baptised into his death? Therefore we have been buried with him by baptism into death, so that, just as Christ was raised from the dead by the glory of the Father, so we too might walk in newness of life.

For if we have been united with him in a death like his, we will certainly be united with him in a resurrection like his. We know that our old self was crucified with him so that the body of sin might be destroyed, and we might no longer be enslaved to sin. For whoever has died is freed from sin. But if we have died with Christ, we believe that we will also live with him. We know that Christ, being raised from the dead, will never die again; death no longer has dominion over him. The death he died, he died to sin, once for all; but the life he lives, he lives to God. So you also must consider yourselves dead to sin and alive to God in Christ Jesus.

Now that you have been freed from sin and enslaved to God, the advantage you get is sanctification. The end is eternal life. For the wages of sin is death, but the free gift of God is eternal life in Christ Jesus our Lord.

Please take a few moments in silence to reflect on the passage, then share a word or phrase that has struck you. Pause to think about what others have said then, after a second reading of the passage, you may wish to share a further thought.

Reflection

Each day, we make choices, establishing priorities in our work and home lives and often times we seek out direction from friends, family members or even spiritual advisors to help us determine how best to tackle a problem, or set in place a plan of action.

When St. John the Baptist was asked, 'what shall we do?' (Luke 3:10-14) by the newly baptised, he encouraged them to radically change their ways – to repent. He counselled them not only to turn to God with a contrite heart but also to firmly resolve to keep the commandments handed down to Moses. In doing so, he was seeking to open their hearts and minds and thus, to prepare them for friendship with Christ who was about to begin his earthly ministry. He was evangelising.

St. John the Baptist may have appeared somewhat eccentric to his fellow countrymen and women. However, the prophet attracted hundreds to the banks of the River Jordan where he baptised each person, cleansing them of their sins in order to begin life anew in the loving embrace of the Lord. Just as God had enlisted John's predecessors, the Old Testament prophets, to gradually bring to light his plan to return humankind to himself, water was again used as a sign, calling God's chosen people to recall their liberation from the slavery of Egypt and to share more deeply into the mysteries of our faith.

Through the mystery of his Incarnation, Christ became man, like us in all things but sin (Hebrews 4:15). Yet, this humble, unassuming man chose to be baptised, not to be cleansed of his own sins but to gather up the sins of all that he would take to his death in order to restore the original holiness bestowed upon our first parents, Adam and Eve (CCC, 405).

Following his baptism, Christ began his earthly ministry. In those three short years, Christ made clear just what we should do – to live by faith, to trust in the Lord and look forward in hope to eternal life with our heavenly Father. While his teaching may have attracted large crowds, Christ did not seek out celebrity status (e.g. Matthew 8:4). Instead, he moved among the people, building personal friendships and curing one-by-one: the bleeding woman, the blind beggar, the paralytic, to mention but a few. Together with his disciples, Christ worked to form a community of believers who listened to his teachings and responded in prayer.

By word and deed, Christ set before us how we should live our lives following our own baptisms when we were cleansed of original sin - dying and rising to live as one with him. Having freely given of himself to enable each of us to share in his divine life, Christ invites each of us to enter into a loving relationship – to freely respond to this wondrous gift. There is no-one better from whom we may seek counsel on how we should live our daily lives.

The Baptism of Jesus by Joachim Patinir (1510-1520)

Has the world and human nature changed so much since the time of Jesus that John the Baptist would give us a different message today? Christ died for our sins, how do we manifest our gratitude? If we see ourselves as sinless can we truly believe that Jesus' death was necessary?

Closing Prayers

You may wish to end this session with some different prayers, the Our Father or silent reflection.

Lord, our God and Father,
through the passion of your Son
you gave us new life.
By our practice of penance
make us one with him in his dying
so that we and all mankind
may be one with him
in his resurrection.
Through Christ our Lord.
Amen.

 Notes

Signpost

This session looked at John the Baptist's ministry, counselling people to repentance as he prepared the way for Jesus Christ. Our own baptism gifts us a share of God's grace as our own sins are washed away but the temptation to sin, our focus for next session, still remains.

What shall we do? Amazing Grace

The Temptation of Christ on the Mountain by Duccio di Buoninsegna (c. 1308-1311)

Reconciled by the Sacraments - Baptism

In essence, the very purpose of Lent is to prepare for the opportunity to renew our baptismal promises at the Easter Vigil. On Holy Saturday evening, in the company of fellow Christians, we turn away from sin and profess our faith. We are asked once again renounce Satan, the glamour of evil and to affirm our belief in the tenets of our faith as set forth in The Creed.

While our efforts through the forty days of Lent are aimed to root out the many forms through which Satan has invaded our hearts and minds in the twenty-first century (i.e. greed, lust, envy, pride, gluttony), we are also reminded that at our baptism, we were liberated from original sin (and in the case of adults personal sins to that time) through the gratuitous love of the Lord. Through his passion, death and resurrection, we were reconciled to God and the promise of eternal life was restored. It is because of our baptism that we call God, 'Our Father' and are able to pray 'lead us not into temptation but deliver us from all evil'.

At our baptism, we were also anointed with the sacred chrism oils to become a temple of the Holy Spirit who prompts us 'to grow in goodness' - 'to believe in God, to hope in him and to love him'. This anointing is repeated at the time of our confirmation to confirm and strengthen our baptismal graces - the gifts of the Holy Spirit that guide our moral life (CCC 1266).

The Resurrection by Francis Hoyland
John 20: 1-18

Definitions - What is Sin?

A sin is a word, deed or intention by which we deliberately and voluntarily offend against the true order of things, as God's loving providence has arranged them. To sin means more than to violate some rules about which men have agreed. Sin turns freely and deliberately against God's love and ignores him. It becomes possible to recognise sin and its seriousness by drawing near to God (YOUCAT, 315).

Lead us not... **Amazing Grace**

Lead us not...

Opening Prayers

Taken from Psalm 73 (72) - to be said all together or the group can divide in half and alternate

All: In the name of the Father, and of the Son, and of the Holy Spirit. Amen.

A: How good God is to Israel,
to those who are pure of heart.

B: Yet my feet came close to stumbling,
my steps had almost slipped
for I was filled with envy of the proud
when I saw how the wicked prosper.

A: And so when my heart grew embittered
and when I was cut to the quick,
I was stupid and did not understand,
no better than a beast in your sight.

B: Yet I was always in your presence;
you were holding me by my right hand.
You will guide me by your counsel
and so you will lead me to glory.

A: To be near God is my happiness.
I have made the Lord God my refuge.
I will tell of your works
at the gates of the city of Zion.

All: Glory be to the Father, and to the Son and to the Holy Spirit. As it was in
the beginning, is now, and ever shall be, world without end. Amen.

*As we come together let us, either aloud or in the silence of our hearts, give thanks
and praise to the Lord for all the things we have accomplished, the joys experienced,
graces received and people met over the past week. Let us also remember all those in
need of our prayers.*

Introduction to the Scripture reading
Let us listen carefully to the Word of the Lord,
and attend to it with the ear of our hearts.
Let us welcome it, and faithfully put it into practice.

St. Benedict of Nursia (c.480-c.547) adapted

Explore the Scriptures Luke 4:1-13
Jesus, full of the Holy Spirit, returned from the Jordan and was led by the Spirit in
the wilderness, where for forty days he was tempted by the devil. He ate nothing
at all during those days, and when they were over, he was famished. The devil said
to him, 'If you are the Son of God, command this stone to become a loaf of bread.'
Jesus answered him, 'It is written, "One does not live by bread alone." '

Then the devil led him up and showed him in an instant all the kingdoms of
the world. And the devil said to him, 'To you I will give their glory and all this
authority; for it has been given over to me, and I give it to anyone I please. If you,
then, will worship me, it will all be yours.' Jesus answered him, 'It is written,
"Worship the Lord your God,
  and serve only him." '

Then the devil took him to Jerusalem, and placed him on the pinnacle of the
temple, saying to him, 'If you are the Son of God, throw yourself down from here,
for it is written,
"He will command his angels concerning you, to protect you", and
"On their hands they will bear you up,
  so that you will not dash your foot against a stone." '
Jesus answered him, 'It is said, "Do not put the Lord your God to the test." ' When
the devil had finished every test, he departed from him until an opportune time.

*Please take a few moments in silence to reflect on the passage, then share a word or
phrase that has struck you. Pause to think about what others have said then, after a
second reading of the passage, you may wish to share a further thought.*

Reflection
Are we victims of our own desires? What control, if any, can we exert over our
baser instincts and ingrained habits? When confronted with a bar of chocolate
can we hold off, or when a job needs to be done do we procrastinate, leaving it
until tomorrow? Perhaps the temptations we face are more serious than these.
Perhaps we face regular and deep-seated challenges to behaving in a manner
that one might expect from a follower of Jesus Christ. St Paul reminds us of
what we should aspire to in his letter to the Christian community at Colossae
(Colossians 3:12-17):

Lead us not... **Amazing Grace**

As God's chosen ones, holy and beloved, clothe yourselves with compassion, kindness, humility, meekness, and patience. Bear with one another and, if anyone has a complaint against another, forgive each other; just as the Lord has forgiven you, so you also must forgive. Above all, clothe yourselves with love, which binds everything together in perfect harmony. Let the peace of Christ rule in your hearts… Let the word of Christ dwell in you richly.

In the early years of the twentieth century, Nobel laureate Ivan Petrovich Pavlov, published his famous work on classical conditioning. In his tests, dogs appeared to respond to the promise of food by salivating when a bell was rung. In a similar way we can find it easy to ignore some of the many stimuli around us and others we will find hard to resist. All too often the temptation is to the opposite of Paul's instructions to the Colossians: we find ourselves drawn to selfishness and spitefulness, to holding on to resentment and impatience. The temptation to sin is a real one and is as deeply ingrained as our desire for the love of God. The Church has a word for this, concupiscence, a holdover from the first sin of pride, selfishness and disobedience (CCC, 2515). It unsettles our ability to avoid sin. As we understand, Jesus gathered all sin to himself on the Cross, dying and rising again for our salvation. Yet despite this once and for all sacrificial and loving act we are still inclined to do wrong, to make mistakes, to miss the standard he has set.

Awareness that we fail is not really a cause for recrimination but a sign of maturity. We should only start to worry we feel that there is little we can do better because we feel helpless, or worse, when we feel that we are doing brilliantly and don't need God's grace (e.g. Luke 18:9-14)! The Second Vatican Council's document on the *Church in the Modern World* talks in terms of the tensions we may feel:

'In man himself many elements wrestle with one another. Thus, on the one hand, as a creature he experiences his limitations in a multitude of ways. On the other, he feels himself to be boundless in his desires and summoned to a higher life. Pulled by manifold attractions, he is constantly forced to choose among them and to renounce some. Indeed, as a weak and sinful being, he often does what he would not, and fails to do what he would. Hence he suffers from internal divisions, and from these flow so many and such great discords in society' (*Gaudium et spes*, 10).

Inspiration and solace can be found, naturally, in the person of Christ. His example in the desert when tempted by power, wealth, food when hungry show not just will power and stamina but trust in God. We should wrestle against the 'manifold attractions' that distract us from God but clearly we are at our strongest when putting ourselves in His hands.

How do you go about resisting temptation? When have you most felt challenged to follow the message of Christ? When have you most felt in the hands of God? Is the call to the Christian life, as we read in St Paul's letter to the Colossians, entirely possible?

Closing Prayers

You may wish to end this session with some different prayers or silent reflection.

Dear Father,
all our hope is in you.
Give us the grace of reconciliation
with you and with each other.
Enlighten our minds, renew our hearts;
give us your strength to heal our weakness,
your power to rekindle our courage.
We aks this through Jesus Christ our Lord.
Amen.

Notes

Signpost

This session looked at very real pull of temptation to sin and to turn from the will of God. We also reflected on the love of God and his desire for us to enter into a deeper relationship with him. The call to conversion, a daily matter and the theme for next session, is ever-present for those who follow Christ.

Lead us not... **Amazing Grace**

The Return of the Prodigal Son by Rembrandt van Rijn (c. 1661-1669)

Reconciled by the Sacraments - Eucharist

Our ongoing conversion is sustained by our active participation in the Eucharist, through which we participate in Christ's redemptive sacrifice and are nourished with the Bread of Life in Holy Communion. It is from the Eucharist that every grace flows as from a fountain of divine charity. As we read in the Second Vatican Council's *Lumen Gentium*: 'In order to reach perfection, the faithful should use the strength dealt out to them by Christ's gift' (LG, 40).

In *Sacramentum Caritatis*, Pope Benedict XVI reminds us of the intrinsic relationship between the Eucharist and the Sacrament of Reconciliation:

'We know that the faithful are surrounded by a culture that tends to eliminate the sense of sin and to promote a superficial approach that overlooks the need to be in a state of grace in order to approach sacramental communion worthily. The loss of a consciousness of sin always entails a certain superficiality in the understanding of God's love. Bringing out the elements within the rite of Mass that express consciousness of personal sin and, at the same time, of God's mercy, can prove most helpful. Furthermore, the relationship between the Eucharist and the sacrament of Reconciliation reminds us that sin is never a purely individual affair; it always damages the ecclesial communion that we have entered through Baptism' (SC, 20).

The Supper at Emmaus by Francis Hoyland
Luke 24: 28-35

Definitions - What is Penance?

Penance is making restitution or satisfaction for a wrong that has been committed. Penance must not take place exclusively in my head; one must express it in acts of charity and in solidarity with others. One does penance also by praying, fasting, and supporting the poor spiritually and materially (YOUCAT, 230).

Continuing conversion **Amazing Grace**

Continuing conversion

Opening Prayers
Taken from Psalm 130 (129) - to be said all together or the group can divide in half and alternate

All: In the name of the Father, and of the Son, and of the Holy Spirit. Amen.

A: Out of the depths I cry to you, O Lord,
Lord, hear my voice!
O let your ears be attentive
to the voice of my pleading.

B: If you, O Lord, should mark our guilt,
Lord, who would survive?
But with you is found forgiveness:
for this we revere you.

A: My soul is waiting for the Lord.
I count on his word.
My soul is longing for the Lord
more than watchman for daybreak.

B: Because with the Lord there is mercy
and fullness of redemption,
Israel indeed he will redeem
from all its iniquity.

All: Glory be to the Father, and to the Son and to the Holy Spirit. As it was in the beginning, is now, and ever shall be, world without end. Amen.

As we come together let us, either aloud or in the silence of our hearts, give thanks and praise to the Lord for all the things we have accomplished, the joys experienced, graces received and people met over the past week. Let us also remember all those in need of our prayers.

Introduction to the Scripture reading
Let us listen carefully to the Word of the Lord,
and attend to it with the ear of our hearts.
Let us welcome it, and faithfully put it into practice.

St. Benedict of Nursia (c.480-c.547) adapted

Explore the Scriptures 1 John 1:1-10

We declare to you what was from the beginning, what we have heard, what we have seen with our eyes, what we have looked at and touched with our hands, concerning the word of life - this life was revealed, and we have seen it and testify to it, and declare to you the eternal life that was with the Father and was revealed to us - we declare to you what we have seen and heard so that you also may have fellowship with us; and truly our fellowship is with the Father and with his Son Jesus Christ. We are writing these things so that our joy may be complete.

This is the message we have heard from him and proclaim to you, that God is light and in him there is no darkness at all. If we say that we have fellowship with him while we are walking in darkness, we lie and do not do what is true; but if we walk in the light as he himself is in the light, we have fellowship with one another, and the blood of Jesus his Son cleanses us from all sin. If we say that we have no sin, we deceive ourselves, and the truth is not in us. If we confess our sins, he who is faithful and just will forgive us our sins and cleanse us from all unrighteousness. If we say that we have not sinned, we make him a liar, and his word is not in us.

Please take a few moments in silence to reflect on the passage, then share a word or phrase that has struck you. Pause to think about what others have said then, after a second reading of the passage, you may wish to share a further thought.

Reflection

In 1939, Alcoholics Anonymous (AA) published *The Story of How More Than One Hundred Men Have Recovered from Alcoholism*. In it could be found the famous twelve-steps, a process for recovery from addiction and compulsion:

- admitting that one cannot control one's addiction or compulsion;
- recognising a higher power that can give strength;
- examining past errors with the help of a sponsor (experienced member);
- making amends for these errors;
- learning to live a new life with a new code of behaviour;
- helping others who suffer from the same addictions or compulsions.

The pattern is a spiritual one, the guiding principles not dissimilar to the call to continuing conversion of any Christian. The AA encourage members to take each day at a time, small steps taken successively can lead a long way. So it is with us as disciples of Christ, each day is an opportunity to recalibrate our compass on God's will, each day is an opportunity to express contrition for our failings and our joy and thanks at the graces we have received. In a religious context we could summarise the twelve-steps as follows:

- admitting that we are inclined to sin;
- recognising God provides us with strength enough to overcome our weak and human nature;
- examining past errors through the sacrament of reconciliation;
- making amends for these errors through acts of penance (prayer, fasting and charitable deeds);
- learning, each day, to live out our baptismal vocation;
- helping others to come to the realisation that Jesus Christ is the way, the truth and the life.

Naturally, we can only really discern what we need to do, where we have gone wrong and what we need to do to make amends if we take the time to reflect. While there may be a nagging sense, perhaps a feeling of guilt, examining our lives in the context of Christ's message of God's love is constantly needed for our spiritual health. While John the Baptist distanced himself from the world and became a 'voice crying out in the wilderness' (John 1:23, Isaiah 40:3) and the Desert Fathers and Mothers – monks, hermits and ascetics – fled to the North African desert to experience solitude, we rarely have the luxury of even a day or two away from the strain and insistence of daily living. St James advised the universal Church to remain 'unstained by the world' (James 1:27) amid the din and sin of the towns and villages of his time. That message is for us too. Life as a faithful child of God is a life daily aspiring to avoid conflict with God's will. The simple fact is that we have each been gifted free will and God – perhaps much to his dismay – respects this utterly. We have the freedom to love and to hate, to embrace and dismiss, to obey and disobey his will.

In preparation for the Second Vatican Council, Pope John XXIII produced a wonderful document expressing his hopes that the Council may bring an 'abundance of light and grace' and 'the dawning of a new and fairer age'. In this document, *Paenitentiam Agere*, he called the Council Fathers and the whole Church to a wider practice of internal repentance and exterior penance. The call to penance, Pope John wrote, requires all Christians to recognise it as 'coming from the divine Redeemer for the purpose of bringing about their spiritual renewal'… to 'make our souls glow in His sight with desire of Him.'

Acts of Penance, traditionally in the form of prayer, fasting and almsgiving - central at Lent but necessary all year around - 'help us to repress our worldly appetites, that we may the more easily obtain the blessings of heaven' (PA, 17).

The sacrament of reconciliation permits us a fresh start and, so too, we can try to make something of the noise and troubles found in the everyday. Perhaps we can try to make each moment holy with a calm and gentle spirit, and see each day as a fresh opportunity to rededicate ourselves to him; performing acts of penance, which seek to remove the obstacles to God's love for us and our love for God. Unlike God's, however, our self-giving is gradual and our conversion - conforming to his will - takes time.

Any sacrament is an encounter with Christ, an encounter which with grace leaves us better off. How do you approach the different sacraments? How open would you say you are to the grace of God?

Closing Prayers
You may wish to end this session with some different prayers or silent reflection.

Heavenly Father,
your Son Jesus gave up everything for his friends.
He spent his life teaching them and helping them,
and eventually he died for them.
Help us to understand the value
of both giving and receiving friendship and forgiveness,
so that we may become more like your Son,
Jesus Christ our Lord.
Amen.

Notes

Signpost

This session looked at our lives in terms of conversion. Each of us is called to reflect on who we are and where we are in terms of our relationship to God. Such a process is continuous as we are drawn to sin and temptation but deeply attracted to God's love. Next session will explore the healing power of this same love.

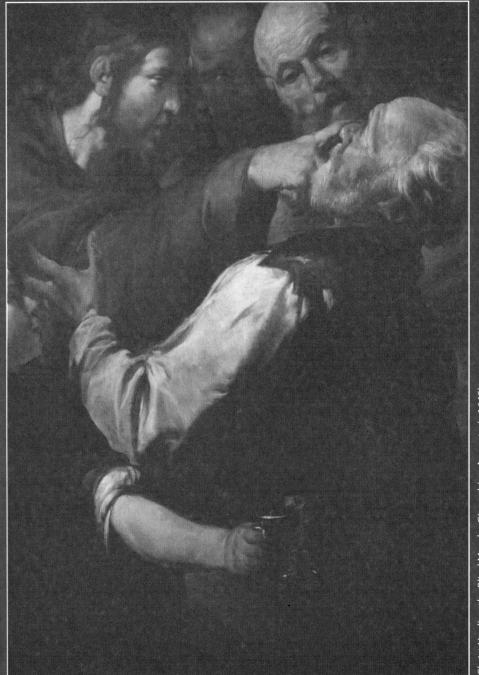

Christ Healing the Blind Man by Gioacchino Assereto (c. 1640)

Reconciled by the Sacraments - Anointing of the Sick

While it is everyone's wish for a long, healthy life, injury or illness can strike at any time. Even those who live to a ripe old age are generally confronted with failing health. Throughout Holy Scripture, we continually read of Christ's contact with the sick and suffering. He laid his hands on them, prayed with them and healed them.

Today, the priest similarly administers the sacrament of Anointing the Sick not just to those about to die but to all those in danger of death from sickness, old age or imminent major surgery. Originally called 'Extreme Unction' until the time of the Second Vatican Council , this sacrament also includes holy anointing to signify 'the grace of the Holy Spirit. [Particularly important for those no longer able to partake of the sacrament of penance,] the anointing removes any remaining sin and its remnants. It brings relief and strength to the soul of the sick person' (*Sacram unctionem infrimorum*).

In the prayers that accompany these gestures, notably known as 'the prayers of faith,' the sick person is united more closely to Christ's passion, death and resurrection. In doing so, 'suffering, a consequence of original sin, acquires new meaning; it becomes a participation in the saving work of Jesus' (CCC, 1521).

Peter's Denial by Francis Hoyland
Matthew 26:69-75; Mark 14:66-72; Luke22:54-71; John18:12-27

Definitions - What is Repentance?

The insight into one's personal guilt produces a longing to better oneself; this is called contrition. We arrive at contrition when we see the contradiction between God's love and our sin. Then we are full of sorrow for our sins; we resolve to change our life and place all our hope in God's help (YOUCAT, 229).

The healing power Amazing **Grace**

The healing power

Opening Prayers

Taken from Psalm 107 (106) - to be said all together or the group can divide in half and alternate

All: In the name of the Father, and of the Son, and of the Holy Spirit. Amen.

A: O give thanks to the Lord for he is good;
for his love endures for ever."

B: Some wandered in the desert, in the wilderness,
finding no way to a city they could dwell in.
Then they cried to the Lord in their need
and he rescued them from their distress

A: Some were sick on account of their sins
and afflicted on account of their guilt.
Then they cried to the Lord in their need
and he rescued them from their distress.

B: Let them thank the Lord for his love,
for the wonders he does for men.
Let them offer a sacrifice of thanks
and tell of his deeds with rejoicing.

A: He pours contempt upon princes,
makes them wander in trackless wastes.
But he raises the needy from distress;
makes families numerous as a flock.

B: The upright see it and rejoice
but all who do wrong are silenced.
Whoever is wise, let him heed these things.
And consider the love of the Lord.

All: Glory be to the Father, and to the Son and to the Holy Spirit. As it was in
the beginning, is now, and ever shall be, world without end. Amen.

As we come together let us, either aloud or in the silence of our hearts, give thanks and praise to the Lord for all the things we have accomplished, the joys experienced, graces received and people met over the past week. Let us also remember all those in need of our prayers.

Introduction to the Scripture reading

Let us listen carefully to the Word of the Lord,
and attend to it with the ear of our hearts.
Let us welcome it, and faithfully put it into practice.

St. Benedict of Nursia (c.480-c.547) adapted

Explore the Scriptures Luke 5:17-26

One day, while he was teaching, Pharisees and teachers of the law were sitting nearby (they had come from every village of Galilee and Judea and from Jerusalem); and the power of the Lord was with him to heal. Just then some men came, carrying a paralysed man on a bed. They were trying to bring him in and lay him before Jesus; but finding no way to bring him in because of the crowd, they went up on the roof and let him down with his bed through the tiles into the middle of the crowd in front of Jesus. When he saw their faith, he said, 'Friend, your sins are forgiven you.' Then the scribes and the Pharisees began to question, 'Who is this who is speaking blasphemies? Who can forgive sins but God alone?'

When Jesus perceived their questionings, he answered them, 'Why do you raise such questions in your hearts? Which is easier, to say, "Your sins are forgiven you", or to say, "Stand up and walk"? But so that you may know that the Son of Man has authority on earth to forgive sins' - he said to the one who was paralysed - 'I say to you, stand up and take your bed and go to your home.' Immediately he stood up before them, took what he had been lying on, and went to his home, glorifying God. Amazement seized all of them, and they glorified God and were filled with awe, saying, 'We have seen strange things today.'

Please take a few moments in silence to reflect on the passage, then share a word or phrase that has struck you. Pause to think about what others have said then, after a second reading of the passage, you may wish to share a further thought.

Reflection

As a child, can you remember waking from a bad dream and heading to your parents' bed? Perhaps you fell in the playground and grazed your knee then sought out a teacher for a plaster and a hug? As an adult have you indulged the need for a bowl of comforting food after a particularly unpleasant journey home or sought the solace of friends after an argument at work? Whether as an adult or as a child we find comfort in the familiar and we long for a sympathetic ear.

The healing power Amazing Grace

Hurt needs healing and when we sin, we cause damage no less severe than physical trauma though much harder to see. Jesus draws our attention to the need for spiritual healing in the passage we have just read. While the Pharisees and their scribes complained to his disciples about his bold claims, Jesus reminded those gathered of his power over sin, going on to assert that 'those who are well have no need of a physician, but those who are sick; I have come to call not the righteous but sinners to repentance' (Luke 5:30-32).

If we are to take Jesus Christ as our model – and we would seem heartily encouraged to do so! – then we must trust that God has not made it impossible. In the way he treats people who come to him, often pompous and frequently poor; the way he heals and helps those in need and the way he lives less for himself than for others culminating with the ultimate sacrifice and deepest love. Jesus' healing action was visible throughout his ministry and in his death and is connected with the intense relationship he had both with his neighbour and with the Father.

As Christians, we often forget that the purpose of Jesus' Incarnation is to both reconcile us to the Father for the sins we have committed and to give us the joyful understanding that we are able to enter into a deeply personal and familial relationship with Almighty God. The sacrament of reconciliation is not to be feared but is a natural extension of this saving love. The sacrament of reconciliation is a gift for the long journey to the Father where we inevitably fall – it is a helping hand in the right direction and when well used, it is liberating – a breath of fresh air and a relief of a burdensome load.

Catholic guilt has become a cliché, one hears that Christians are widely held to be a joyless bunch of rule-bound bigots. We shouldn't recognise ourselves in this. Faith is to be lived out and expressed in a freeing and joyous manner. Anything that helps us to move closer to the source of all joy, to God who is love (1 John 4:8), should be accepted not just with one hand but with both!

Forgiveness can sometimes take a long time but how open are you to being an agent of forgiveness? Is your life as a Christian characterised by joy? How would you describe your attitude to the sacrament of reconciliation - is it one of fear or enthusiasm?

Closing Prayers
You may wish to end this session with some different prayers or silent reflection.

Father in heaven,
through your Son Jesus you showed the world
that no sin is too great to be forgiven.
We open ourselves up to your love
so that what is evil in us will be destroyed
and that what is good in us will grow
into a reflection of your glory.
We make our prayer with him who was raised to glory,
Jesus Christ our Lord.
Amen.

 Notes

Signpost
This session looked at the healing we can feel through being forgiven and through the contrition expressed and absolution received in the sacrament of reconciliation. The next season of faith-sharing will explore prayer and spirituality, how we express the love and gratitude we feel for God's gift of salvation through Christ Jesus.

Daily Prayer
Sunday to Saturday

The daily prayers on the following pages are drawn from the Divine Office (Liturgy of the Hours). Each day contains a hymn, a Scripture reading, a psalm or Old Testament canticle and a selection of prayers taken from the days of Lent.

Together with the Mass, the Divine Office (Liturgy of the Hours) constitutes the official public prayer life of the Church. It is celebrated, under different names, in both the Eastern and Western Churches. The Divine Office is intended to be read communally but here we invite you to use it as a personal daily prayer.

'The Office is... the prayer not only of the clergy but of the whole People of God.'

Apostolic Constitution, Canticum Laudis

Sunday - Seeking Salvation

Introduction

O God, come to our aid. Lord, make haste to help us.

Glory be to the Father and to the Son and to the Holy Spirit, as it was in the beginning, is now, and ever shall be, world without end. Amen. (Alleluia)

omit Alleluias during Lent

Hymn

Be thou my vision, O Lord of my heart,
Be all else naught to me, save that thou art;
Thou my best thought in the day and the
  night,
Both waking and sleeping, thy presence
  my light.

Be thou my wisdom, be thou my true word,
Be thou ever with me, and I with thee Lord;
Be thou my great Father, and I thy true son;
Be thou in me dwelling, and I with thee
  one.

Riches I heed not, nor man's empty praise:
Be thou mine inheritance now and always;
Be thou and thou only the first in my heart;
O Sovereign of Heaven, my treasure thou
  art.

High King of Heaven, thou Heaven's
  bright sun,
O grant me its joys after victory is won!;
Great heart of my own heart, whatever
  befall,
Still be my vision, O Ruler of all.

Antiphon

This is the time of repentance for us to atone for our sins and seek salvation.

Psalmody

Psalm 112 (113)

Praise, O servants of the Lord,
praise the name of the Lord!
May the name of the Lord be blessed
both now and for evermore!
From the rising of the sun to its setting
praised be the name of the Lord!

High above all nations is the Lord,
above the heavens his glory.
Who is like the Lord, our God,
who has risen on high to his throne
yet stoops from the heights to look down,
to look down upon heaven and earth?

From the dust he lifts up the lowly,
from the dungheap he raises the poor
to set them in the company of princes,
yes, with the princes of his people.
To the childless wife he gives a home
and gladdens her heart with children.

Glory be…

Antiphon

This is the time of repentance for us to atone for our sins and seek salvation.

Reading

2 Corinthians 6:1-4

We urge this appeal upon you: you have received the grace of God; do not let it go for nothing. God's own words are: In the hour of my favour I gave heed to you, on the day of deliverance I came to your aid. The hour of favour has now come; now, I say, has the day of deliverance dawned. In order that our service may not be brought into discredit, we avoid giving offence in anything. As God's servants, we try to recommend ourselves in all circumstances.

Short Responsory
℟ Hear us, Lord, and have mercy, for we have sinned against you.
℣ Listen, Christ, to the prayers of those who cry to you.
Glory be…

Benedictus/Magnificat Antiphon
God loved the world so much that he gave his only Son, so that everyone who believes in him may not be lost but may have eternal life.

Benedictus (if said in the morning) or Magnificat (if said in the evening) - see inside front cover for these prayers

Intercessions
Let us give glory to Christ the Lord. He is our master, our example and our brother.

℟ Lord, give life to your people.

Lord Jesus, you became a man like us in every way, but did not sin; may we open our lives to others, share their laughter and tears, and grow day by day in love.
℟ Lord, give life to your people.

Let us serve you in the hungry and give you to eat; let us see you in the thirsty and give you to drink.

℟ Lord, give life to your people.

May we live up to the example of Mary and the saints; may we follow you more perfectly in everything.

℟ Lord, give life to your people.

Our Father…

Concluding prayer
God our Father,
you bid us listen to your Son,
the well-beloved.
Nourish our hearts on your word,
purify the eyes of our mind,
and fill us with joy at the vision of your glory.
We make our prayer through Jesus Christ our Lord.
Amen.

Let us go forward in peace, our eyes upon heaven, the only one goal of our labours.
St Thérèse of Lisieux

Monday - Praying for Grace

Introduction
O God, come to our aid. Lord, make haste to help us.

Glory be to the Father and to the Son and to the Holy Spirit, as it was in the beginning, is now, and ever shall be, world without end. Amen. (Alleluia)

omit Alleluias during Lent

Hymn
Praise to the Holiest in the height,
And in the depth be praise;
In all His words most wonderful,
Most sure in all His ways.

O loving wisdom of our God!
When all was sin and shame,
A second Adam to the fight
And to the rescue came.

O wisest love! that flesh and blood,
Which did in Adam fail,
Should strive afresh against the foe,
Should strive and should prevail.

And that a higher gift than grace
Should flesh and blood refine,
God's Presence and His very Self,
And Essence all divine.

And in the garden secretly,
And on the Cross on high,
Should teach His brethren, and inspire
To suffer and to die.

Praise to the Holiest in the height,
And in the depth be praise;
In all His words most wonderful,
Most sure in all His ways.

Antiphon
To me life is Christ, and death gain. I will glory in the cross of my Lord Jesus Christ.

Psalmody
Psalm 19 (18)

The law of the Lord is perfect,
it revives the soul.
The rule of the Lord is to be trusted,
it gives wisdom to the simple.

The precepts of the Lord are right,
they gladden the heart.
The command of the Lord is clear,
it gives light to the eyes.

The fear of the Lord is holy,
abiding for ever.
The decrees of the Lord are truth
and all of them just.

They are more to be desired than gold,
than the purest of gold
and sweeter are they than honey,
than honey from the comb.

So in them your servant finds instruction;
great reward is in their keeping.
But who can detect all his errors?
From hidden faults acquit me.

From presumption restrain your servant
and let it not rule me.
Then shall I be blameless,
clean from grave sin.

May the spoken words of my mouth,
the thoughts of my heart,
win favour in your sight, O Lord,
my rescuer, my rock!

Glory be...

Antiphon

To me life is Christ, and death gain. I will glory in the cross of my Lord Jesus Christ.

Reading
Wisdom 11:24-25

You are merciful to all, Lord, because you can do all things and overlook men's sins so that they can repent. Yes, you love all that exists, you hold nothing of what you have made in abhorrence.

Short Responsory

℟ From my sins turn away your face.
℣ And blot out my guilt.
Glory be…

Benedictus/Magnificat Antiphon

Be compassionate as your Father is compassionate, says the Lord.

Benedictus (if said in the morning) or Magnificat (if said in the evening) - see inside front cover for these prayers

Intercessions

Let us praise God the Father, who hears the prayers of his children and grants what they ask.

℟ Lord, have mercy on your people.

Lord on Sinai, you gave the law to Moses and completed it through Christ; write your law in the hearts of all that they may be faithful to your covenant.

℟ Lord, have mercy on your people.

Help us to create a community where people care for one another; let us work together for the good of all.

℟ Lord, have mercy on your people.

May children grow strong in grace; may the young advance in your love.

℟ Lord, have mercy on your people.

Our Father…

Concluding prayer

Lord God,
you give the world new life
by mysteries which are beyond our grasp.
May your Church not be deprived of earthly help
while she makes progress by the strength of those eternal gifts.
We make our prayer through
  Christ our Lord.
Amen.

Let us go forward in peace, our eyes upon heaven, the only one goal of our labours.
St Thérèse of Lisieux

Tuesday - Seventy times seven

Introduction

O God, come to our aid. Lord, make haste to help us.

Glory be to the Father and to the Son and to the Holy Spirit, as it was in the beginning, is now, and ever shall be, world without end. Amen. (Alleluia)

omit Alleluias during Lent

Hymn

Love divine, all loves excelling,
Joy of heaven to earth come down;
Fix in us thy humble dwelling;
All thy faithful mercies crown!
Jesus, Thou art all compassion,
Pure unbounded love Thou art;
Visit us with Thy salvation;
Enter every trembling heart.

Breathe, O breathe Thy loving Spirit,
Into every troubled breast!
Let us all in Thee inherit;
Let us find that second rest.
Take away our bent to sinning;
Alpha and Omega be;
End of faith, as its Beginning,
Set our hearts at liberty.

Finish, then, Thy new creation;
Pure and spotless let us be.
Let us see Thy great salvation
Perfectly restored in Thee;
Changed from glory into glory,
Till in heaven we take our place,
Till we cast our crowns before Thee,
Lost in wonder, love, and praise.

Antiphon

My heavenly Father will deal the same way with you if you do not forgive your brother from your heart.

Psalmody

Psalm 21(20)

O Lord, your strength gives joy to the
   King;
how your saving help makes him glad!
You have granted him his heart's desire;
you have not refused the prayer of his lips.

You came to meet him with the blessings
   of success,
you have set on his head a crown of pure
   gold.
He asked you for life and this you have given,
days that will last from age to age.

Your saving help has given him glory.
You have laid upon him majesty and
   splendour,
you have granted your blessings to him
   forever.
You have made him rejoice with the joy of
   your presence.

For you will force them to retreat;
at them you will aim with your bow.
O Lord, arise in your strength;
we shall sing and praise your power.

Glory be...

Antiphon

My heavenly Father will deal the same way with you if you do not forgive your brother from your heart.

Amazing Grace

Reading   *Joel 2:12-13*

Come back to me with all your heart,
fasting, weeping, mourning. Let your
hearts be broken, not your garments torn;
turn to the Lord your God again, for he is
all tenderness and compassion, slow to
anger, rich in graciousness, and ready to
relent.

Short Responsory

℟ It is he who will free me from the snare
of the hunters.
℣ And from the evil word.
Glory be…

Benedictus/Magnificat Antiphon

Peter, I do not tell you to forgive seven
times, but seventy time seven, said the
Lord.

Benedictus (if said in the morning)
or Magnificat (if said in the evening) -
see inside front cover for these prayers

Intercessions

Let us pray earnestly to Christ the Lord.
He tells us to watch and pray that we may
not fall into temptation.

℟ Hear us, Lord, and have mercy.

Lord Jesus, you promised to be with those
who are gathered in your name; keep us
united with you as we pray to the Father
in the Holy Spirit.

℟ Hear us, Lord, and have mercy.

Help us to care for our neighbour and
show your love for all; through us let the
light of your salvation shine in the world.

℟ Hear us, Lord, and have mercy.

Our Father…

Concluding prayer

Lord, be the beginning and end
of all that we do and say.
Prompt our actions with your grace,
and complete them with your all-
powerful help.
Through Christ our Lord.
Amen.

Let us go forward in peace, our eyes upon
heaven, the only one goal of our labours.
St Thérèse of Lisieux

Wednesday - Even to the shedding of blood

Introduction
O God, come to our aid. Lord, make haste to help us.

Glory be to the Father and to the Son and to the Holy Spirit, as it was in the beginning, is now, and ever shall be, world without end. Amen. (Alleluia)

omit Alleluias during Lent

Hymn
The king of love my shepherd is,
Whose goodness faileth never;
I nothing lack if I am his
And he is mine for ever.

Where streams of living water flow
My ransomed soul he leadeth,
And where the verdant pastures grow
With food celestial feedeth.

Perverse and foolish oft I strayed,
But yet in love he sought me,
And on his shoulder gently laid,
And home rejoicing brought me.

In death's dark vale I fear no ill
With thee, dear Lord, beside me;
Thy rod and staff my comfort still,
Thy cross before to guide me.

Thou spread'st a table in my sight;
Thy unction grace bestoweth;
And O what transport of delight
From thy pure chalice floweth!

And so through all the length of days
Thy goodness faileth never:
Good shepherd, may I sing thy praise
Within thy house for ever.

Antiphon
This is the time of repentance for us to atone for our sins and seek salvation.

Psalmody
Psalm 119 (118): 9-16 II Beth

How shall the young remain sinless?
By obeying your word.
I have sought you with all my heart;
let me not stray from your commands.

I treasure your promise in my heart
lest I sin against you.
Blessed are you, O Lord;
teach me your statutes.

With my tongue I have recounted
the decrees of your lips.
I rejoiced to do your will
as they all riches were mine.

I will ponder all your precepts
and consider your paths.
I take delight in your statutes;
I will not forget your word.

Antiphon
This is the time of repentance for us to atone for our sins and seek salvation.

Reading
Philippians 2:12-15

Keep on working, with fear and trembling, to complete your salvation, for God is always at work in you to make you willing and able to obey his own purpose. do everything without complaining or arguing, that you may be innocent and pure, as God's perfect children.

Amazing Grace

Short responsory
℟ A pure heart create for me, O God.
℣ Put a steadfast spirit within me.

Glory be…

Benedictus/Magnificat Antiphon
The Son of Man will be handed over to the Gentiles to be mocked and scourged and crucified; and on the third day he will rise again.

Benedictus (if said in the morning) or Magnificat (if said in the evening) - see inside front cover for these prayers

Intercessions
God our Father knows all the needs of his people, but he wants to give first place to his kingdom. Let us proclaim his greatness in our prayer.

℟ May your kingdom come in all its justice.

Holy Father, you gave us Christ as the shepherd of our souls; may your people always have priests who care for them with his great love.

℟ May your kingdom come in all its justice.

Help those who do not believe in the gospel to come into your Church; build it up in love to manifest your goodness everywhere.

℟ May your kingdom come in all its justice.

Our Father…

Concluding prayer
Lord God,
you crown the merits of the saints
and pardon sinners when they repent.
Forgive us our sins, now that we come before you,
humbly confessing our guilt.
Through Christ our Lord.
Amen.

Let us go forward in peace, our eyes upon heaven, the only one goal of our labours.
St Thérèse of Lisieux

Thursday - Standing firm in the Lord

O God, come to our aid. Lord, make haste to help us.

Glory be to the Father and to the Son and to the Holy Spirit, as it was in the beginning, is now, and ever shall be, world without end. Amen. (Alleluia)

omit Alleluias during Lent

Hymn
There is a green hill far away,
Outside a city wall,
Where the dear Lord was crucified,
Who died to save us all.

We may not know, we cannot tell,
What pains He had to bear;
But we believe it was for us
He hung and suffered there.

He died that we might be forgiv'n,
He died to make us good,
That we might go at last to Heav'n,
Saved by His precious blood.

There was no other good enough
To pay the price of sin;
He only could unlock the gate
Of heaven and let us in.

O dearly, dearly has He loved,
And we must love Him, too,
And trust in His redeeming blood,
And try His works to do.

Antiphon
Armed with justice which is the power of God, let us prove ourselves with great patience.

Psalmody

Psalm 25 (24)

To you, O Lord, I lift up my soul.
I trust you, let me not be disappointed;
do not let my enemies triumph.
Those who hope in you shall not be disappointed,
but only those who wantonly break faith.

Lord, make me know your ways.
Lord, teach me your paths.
Make me walk in your truth, and teach me:
for you are God my saviour.

In you I hope all day long
because of your goodness, O Lord.
Remember your mercy, Lord,
and the love you have shown from of old.
Do not remember the sins of my youth.
In your love remember me.

The Lord is good and upright.
He shows the path to those who stray,
He guides the humble in the right path,
He teaches his way to the poor.

His ways are faithfulness and love
for those who keep his covenant and law.
Lord, for the sake of your name
forgive my guilt, for it is great.

Antiphon
Armed with justice which is the power of God, let us prove ourselves with great patience.

Reading
James 4:7-8, 10

Be God's true subjects; stand firm against the devil, and he will run away from you; come close to God, and he will come close to you. You that are sinners must wash your hands clean, you that are in two minds must purify the intention of your hearts. Humble yoursleves before the Lord and he will exalt you.

Short Responsory
℟ I said: 'Lord, have mercy on me.'
℣ 'Heal my soul for I have sinned against you.'
Glory be…

Benedictus/Magnificat Antiphon
Ask, and it will be given to you; seek, and you will find; knock, and the door will be opened to you.

Benedictus (if said in the morning) or Magnificat (if said in the evening) - see inside front cover for these prayers

Intercessions
Let us pray to Christ the Lord, who gave us the new commandment to love one another.
℟ Lord, may your people grow in love.

You interceded with the Father for those who nailed you on the Cross; help us to love our enemies and pray for those who injure us.
℟ Lord, may your people grow in love.

Though the mystery of your body and blood deepen our courage and faith, strengthen the weak, comfort the sorrowful and fill the dying with new hope.
℟ Lord, may your people grow in love.

Light of the world, you gave sight to the man born blind; enlighten us in baptism through the washing in water and the word of life.
℟ Lord, may your people grow in love.

Our Father...

Concluding prayer
Lord God,
you love innocence of heart,
and when it is lost you alone can restore it.
Turn then our hearts to you,
and kindle in them the fire of your Spirit,
so that we may be steadfast in faith
and unwearied in good works.
Through Christ our Lord,
Amen.

Let us go forward in peace, our eyes upon heaven, the only one goal of our labours.
St Thérèse of Lisieux

Friday - Breaking the bonds of sin

Introduction
O God, come to our aid. Lord, make haste to help us.

Glory be to the Father and to the Son and to the Holy Spirit, as it was in the beginning, is now, and ever shall be, world without end. Amen. (Alleluia)

omit Alleluias during Lent

Hymn
Lord Jesus, think on me
And purge away my sin;
From earthborn passions set me free
And make me pure within.

Lord Jesus, think on me
Amid the battle's strife;
In all my pain and misery
Be Thou my Health and Life.

Lord Jesus, think on me
Nor let me go astray;
Through darkness and perplexity
Point Thou the heavenly way.

Lord Jesus, think on me
When floods the tempest high;
When on doth rush the enemy,
O Savior, be Thou nigh!

Lord Jesus, think on me
That, when the flood is past,
I may th'eternal brightness see
And share Thy joy at last.

Lord Jesus, think on me
That I may sing above
To Father, Spirit, and to Thee
The strains of praise and love.

Antiphon
Christ the Lord was tempted and suffered for us. Come, let is adore him.

Psalmody
Psalm 51 (50)
Have mercy on me, God, in your kindness.
In your compassion blot out my offence.
O wash me more and more from my guilt
and cleanse me from my sin.

My offences truly I know them;
my sin is always before me
Against you, you alone, have I sinned;
what is evil in your sight I have done.

That you may be justified when you give sentence
and be without reproach when you judge,
O see, in guilt I was born,
a sinner was I conceived.

Indeed you love truth in the heart;
then in the secret of my heart teach me wisdom.
O purify me, then I shall be clean;
O wash me, I shall be whiter than snow.

Make me hear rejoicing and gladness,
that the bones you have crushed may thrill.
From my sins turn away your face
and blot out all my guilt.

Antiphon
Christ the Lord was tempted and suffered for us. Come, let is adore him.

Reading
Isaiah 53:4-5

Ours were the sufferings he bore, ours the sorrows he carried. But we, we thought of him as someone punished, struck by God, and brought low. He was pierced through for our faults, crushed for our sins. On him lies a punishment that brings peace, and through his wounds we are healed.

Short Responsory
℟ My sacrifice is a contrite spirit.
℣ A humbled, contrite spirit you will not spurn, O God.
Glory be…

Benedictus/Magnificat Antiphon
I have done many good works for you to see, says the Lord; for which of these good works do you wish to kill me?

Benedictus (if said in the morning)
or Magnificat (if said in the evening) -
see inside front cover for these prayers

Intercessions
We give thanks to Christ the Lord, who died on the cross that we might live. Let us pray to him with all our heart.

℟ Lord Jesus, may your death bring us to life.

Master and Saviour, you have taught us by your life and renewed us by your passion; do not allow us to grow used to sin.

℟ Lord Jesus, may your death bring us to life.

May we accept from your hands this day, may we make it yours by deeds of love.

℟ Lord Jesus, may your death bring us to life.

End the rebellion within our hearts; make us generous and willing to share.

℟ Lord Jesus, may your death bring us to life.

Our Father…

Concluding prayer
Lord,
break the bonds of sin
which our weaknesses have forged to enchain us,
and in your loving mercy forgive your people's guilt.
We make our prayer through Christ our Lord.
Amen.

Let us go forward in peace, our eyes upon heaven, the only one goal of our labours.
St Thérèse of Lisieux

Saturday - Healing grace

Introduction
O God, come to our aid. Lord, make haste to help us.

Glory be to the Father and to the Son and to the Holy Spirit, as it was in the beginning, is now, and ever shall be, world without end. Amen. (Alleluia)

omit Alleluias during Lent

Hymn
Lord Jesus, as we turn from sin
with strength and hope restored,
receive the homage that we bring
to you our risen Lord.

We call on you whose living word
has made the Father known,
O Shepherd, we have wondered far,
find us and lead us home.

Your glance at Peter helped him know
the love he had denied,
now gaze on us and heal us, Lord,
of selfishness and pride.

Reach out and touch with healing pow'r
the wounds we have received,
that in forgiveness we may love
and may no longer grieve.

Then stay with us when ev'ning comes
and darkness makes us blind,
O stay until the light of dawn
may fill both heart and mind.

Ralph Wright OSB

Antiphon
As I live, says the Lord, I have no pleasure in the death of the wicked man, rather let him turn from his evil way and live.

Psalmody
Psalm 119 (118): 145-152 XIX Koph

I call with all my heart; Lord, hear me,
I will keep your statutes.
I call upon you, save me
and I will do your will.

I rise before dawn and cry for help,
I hope in your word.
My eyes watch through the night
to ponder your promise.

In your love hear my voice, O Lord;
give me life by your decrees.
Those who harm me unjustly draw near;
they are far from your law.

But you, O Lord, are close,
your commands are truth.
Long have I known that your will
is established for ever.

Antiphon
As I live, says the Lord, I have no pleasure in the death of the wicked man, rather let him turn from his evil way and live.

Reading
Isaiah 1:16-18

Wash, make yourselves clean, take your wrong-doing out of my sight. Cease to do evil. Learn to do good, search for justice, help the oppressed, be just to the orphan, plead for the widow. Come now, let us talk this over says the Lord: though your sins are like scarlet, they shall be white as snow; though thye are red as crimson, they shall be like wool.

Short responsory

℟ It is he who will free me from the snare of the hunters.
℣ And from the evil word.
Glory be…

Benedictus/Magnificat Antiphon

The tax collector stood afar off and did not dare to raise his eyes to heaven. He beat his breast and said, 'God, be merciful to me, a sinner.'

Benedictus (if said in the morning) or Magnificat (if said in the evening) - see inside front cover for these prayers

Intercessions

Christ has made us a new creation. He gives us a new birth in the waters of baptism and nourishes us with his word and his body. Let us glorify him in our prayer.

℟ Renew us, Lord, by your grace.

Jesus, you are gentle and humble in spirit; grant us something of your pity, something of your kindness and something of your patience towards all.

℟ Renew us, Lord, by your grace.

Teach us to be neighbours to the sad and the needy; let us imitate you, the good Samaritan.

℟ Renew us, Lord, by your grace.

Grant us the gift of your mercy, pardon our sins and save us from punishment.

℟ Renew us, Lord, by your grace.

Our Father…

Concluding prayer

Lord God,
you have prepared fitting remedies
for our weaknesses;
grant that we may reach out gladly
for your healing grace and
therby live in accordance with your will.
We make our prayer through Christ our
  Lord.
Amen.

Let us go forward in peace, our eyes upon heaven, the only one goal of our labours.

St Thérèse of Lisieux

Supplementary
resources

- More Quotes
- Examinations of Conscience
- Celebrating the Sacrament
- Further reading

More Quotes

My own sin will not hinder the working of God's goodness.

Julian of Norwich (1342–c.1416)

Sin always wounds the sinner.

Caryll Houselander (1901–1954), The Reed of God

Like hairs on the head, mortal man is joined to Jesus Christ, the head of all, but they are full of transgressions and sins because of man's delight in the flesh. But the Church regenerates and purifies these from the unclean stench and filth of sin by penitence and confession, just as hair is cleansed from dew and drops, and as dust is shaken out and cleansed from wool.

Hildegard Of Binden (1098–1179)

God had one son on earth without sin, but never one without suffering.

Augustine of Hippo (354 – 430)

 Watch for your life's sake. Let not your lamps be quenched, nor your loins unloosed; but be ready, for you know not the hour in which our Lord comes. But you shall assemble together often, seeking the things which are befitting to your souls: for the whole time of your faith will not profit you, if you be not made complete in the last time.

The Didache

Of how much greater faith and salutary fear are they who . . . confess their sins to the priests of God in a straightforward manner and in sorrow, making an open declaration of conscience. . . . I beseech you, brethren, let everyone who has sinned confess his sin while he is still in this world, while his confession is still admissible, while the satisfaction and remission made through the priests are still pleasing before the Lord.

Cyprian of Carthage (c.200-258)

Regarding confession, some] flee from this work as being an exposure of themselves, or they put it off from day to day. I presume they are more mindful of modesty than of salvation, like those who contract a disease in the more shameful parts of the body and shun making themselves known to the physicians; and thus they perish along with their own bashfulness.

Tertullian (c. 160 – c. 225)

It is necessary to confess our sins to those to whom the dispensation of God's mysteries is entrusted. Those doing penance of old are found to have done it before the saints. It is written in the Gospel that they confessed their sins to John the Baptist (Matthew 3:6), but in Acts (19:18) they confessed to the apostles.

Basil the Great (329-379)

And pray without ceasing in behalf of other men; for there is hope of the repentance, that they may attain to God. For cannot he that falls arise again, and he may attain to God?

Ignatius of Antioch (c.35-50 - c.98-117)

A man can no more diminish God's glory by refusing to worship Him than a lunatic can put out the sun by scribbling the word, 'darkness' on the walls of his cell.

C.S. Lewis (1898 – 1963), The Problem of Pain

The soul can split the sky in two and let the face of God shine through.

Edna St. Vincent Millay (1892-1950)

Confess your sins in church, and do not go up to your prayer with an evil conscience. This is the way of life. . . . On the Lord's Day gather together, break bread, and give thanks, after confessing your transgressions so that your sacrifice may be pure.

The Didache

You shall judge righteously. You shall not make a schism, but you shall pacify those that contend by bringing them together. You shall confess your sins. You shall not go to prayer with an evil conscience. This is the way of light.

The Letter of Barnabas

[The bishop conducting the ordination of the new bishop shall pray:] God and Father of our Lord Jesus Christ. . . . Pour forth now that power which comes from you, from your royal Spirit, which you gave to your beloved Son, Jesus Christ, and which he bestowed upon his holy apostles . . . and grant this your servant, whom you have chosen for the episcopate, [the power] to feed your holy flock and to serve without blame as your high priest, ministering night and day to propitiate unceasingly before your face and to offer to you the gifts of your holy Church, and by the Spirit of the high priesthood to have the authority to forgive sins, in accord with your command.

Hippolytus (170 – 235)

Read the Psalms - in particular: 4, 23, 37, 41, 51, 103, 136 and 145.

Amazing Grace

You [priests], then, who are disciples of our illustrious physician [Christ], you ought not deny a curative to those in need of healing. And if anyone uncovers his wound before you, give him the remedy of repentance. And he that is ashamed to make known his weakness, encourage him so that he will not hide it from you. And when he has revealed it to you, do not make it public, lest because of it the innocent might be reckoned as guilty by our enemies and by those who hate us.

Aphraahat the Persian Sage (c.270-c.350)

Priests have received a power which God has given neither to angels nor to archangels. It was said to them: 'Whatsoever you shall bind on earth shall be bound in heaven; and whatsoever you shall loose, shall be loosed.'

John Chrysostom (c.347–407)

When you shall have been baptized, keep to a good life in the commandments of God so that you may preserve your baptism to the very end.

Augustine of Hippo (354 – 430)

Among the attributes of God, although they are all equal, mercy shines with even more brilliancy than justice.

Miguel de Cervantes (1547-1616)

People are often unreasonable and self-centered. Forgive them anyway.
If you are kind, people may accuse you of ulterior motives. Be kind anyway.
If you are honest, people may cheat you. Be honest anyway.
If you find happiness, people may be jealous. Be happy anyway.
The good you do today may be forgotten tomorrow. Do good anyway.
Give the world the best you have and it may never be enough. Give your best anyway. For you see, in the end, it is between you and God. It was never between you and them anyway."

Mother Teresa (1910–1997)

To be a Christian means to forgive the inexcusable because God has forgiven the inexcusable in you.

C.S. Lewis (1898 – 1963)

Forgiveness is the name of love practiced among people who love poorly. The hard truth is that all people love poorly. We need to forgive and be forgiven every day, every hour increasingly. That is the great work of love among the fellowship of the weak that is the human family.

Henri J.M. Nouwen (1932-1996)

Examinations of Conscience

An examination of conscience can take a variety of forms. Some people may look closely at the Ten Commandments and 'check off their life' in the context of each Commandment. Others may choose to reflect on a passage of Scripture such as the Sermon on the Mount (Matthew 5) or another passage. Here are some options but feel free to explore what may work for you.

Seven Last Words
The seven last words form part of a Christian meditation that is often used during Lent, Holy Week and Good Friday. The traditional order of the sayings is:

1. Father forgive them, for they know not what they do (Luke 23:34).
2. Truly, I say to you, today you will be with me in paradise (Luke 23:43).
3. Woman, behold your son: behold your mother (John 19:26-27).
4. My God, My God, why have you forsaken me, (Matthew 27:46 and Mark 15:34).
5. I thirst (John 19:28).
6. It is finished (John 19:30).
7. Father, into your hands I commit my spirit (Luke 23:46).

Reflect on each in the context of your life as a follower of Christ. Traditionally, these seven sayings are called words of 1. Forgiveness, 2. Salvation, 3. Relationship, 4. Abandonment, 5. Distress, 6. Triumph and 7. Reunion.

A Prayerful Reflection on the Beatitudes
Based on Matthew 5:1-12

'Blessed are the poor in spirit, for theirs is the kingdom of heaven.'
Keep us from being preoccupied with money and worldly goods, and with trying to increase them at the expense of justice.

'Blessed are the gentle, for they shall inherit the earth.'
Help us not to be ruthless with one another, and to eliminate the discord and violence that exists in the world around us.

'Blessed are those who mourn, for they shall be comforted.'
Let us not be impatient under our own burdens and unconcerned about the burdens of others.

'Blessed are those who hunger and thirst for justice, for they shall be filled.'
Make us thirst for you, the fountain of all holiness, and actively spread your influence in our private lives and in society.

'Blessed are the merciful, for they shall receive mercy.'
Grant that we may be quick to forgive and slow to condemn.

'Blessed are the clean of heart, for they shall see God.'
Free us from our senses and our evil desires, and help us to fix our eyes on you.

'Blessed are the peacemakers, for they shall be called children of God.'
Aid us to make peace in our families, in our country, and in the world.

'Blessed are those who are persecuted for the sake of justice,
for the kingdom of heaven in theirs.'
Make us willing to suffer for the sake of right rather than to practice injustice; and do not let us discriminate against our neighbours and oppress and persecute them.

The Ten Commandments
For a version of an examination of conscience based on the Ten Commandments can be found at: http://www.theworkofgod.org/Library/examine.htm

1. I am the Lord your God, you shall have no other gods before me, you shall not make for yourself an idol
2. You shall not make wrongful use of the name of your God
3. Remember the Sabbath and keep it holy
4. Honour your Father and Mother
5. You shall not murder
6. You shall not commit adultery
7. You shall not steal
8. You shall not bear false witness against your neighbour
9. You shall not covet your neighbour's house
10. You shall not covet your neighbour's wife

Celebrating the Sacrament

After a thorough examination of conscience, the Penitent approaches the Sacrament of Reconciliation. You must have both true contrition (be truly sorry), and a firm resolve to amend one's life.

The Penitent begins:
'In the Name of the Father, and of the Son, and of the Holy Spirit, Amen. Bless me, Father, for I have sinned. It has been (how long?) since my last confession. These are my sins...'

The purpose of saying how long since the last confession, and your state in life is to provide the priest some context and an idea of how you might be looking to approach the sacrament.

Tell the priest your sins. A good confession means confessing all the sins you remember, since your last confession, including the number of times any mortal sins were committed.

Careful reflection on your life and how you might express your relationship to God and any sins or barriers to grace is important. The sacrament is not counselling nor is a rattled of list particularly helpful.

After confessing all your sins, say: 'For these and all my sins, I am truly sorry'.

The priest may discuss your confession with you and then gives you a penance to be said later and asks you to say an Act of Contrition, there are two examples below.

After you have said an Act of Contrition the priest then gives you Absolution, forgiving all sins committed since your last confession. The priest may finish by saying 'Go in peace' or something similar.

There is no need to use these exact words, they are here as a help and a suggestion. If you are unsure what to say or what to do, please ask the priest for help. The Priest is there to help you through this celebration to grow in your love for God. Many 'Confessional Boxes' offer an option of sitting behind a screen or in front of the priest. You may choose whatever you prefer.

O my God, because you are so good.
I am very sorry that I have sinned against you;
and with your help I will try not to sin again. Amen.

I love you Jesus, my love above all things,
I repent with my whole heart for having offended you.
Never permit me to separate myself from you again
Grant that I may always love you
and then do with me what you will.

Further Reading

Joseph Ratzinger (1995) *In the Beginning: A Catholic Understanding of the Story of Creation and the Fall*, W.B. Eerdmans Publishing Company

Scott Hahn (1998) *A Father Who Keeps His Promises: God's Covenant Love in Scripture*, Servant Books

Scott Hahn (2003) *Lord, Have Mercy: The Healing Power of Confession*, Darton, Longman & Todd Ltd

Pope Benedict XVI (2008) *Jesus of Nazareth - volume 1*, Bloomsbury

Timothy Radcliffe (2012) *Take the Plunge: Living Baptism and Confirmation*, Burns and Oates

The New Penance Book, CTS [http://www.cts-online.org.uk/acatalog/info_1_D660.html]

Why go to Confession, CTS

Confession Advice and Encouragement from Pope Benedict XVI (CTS)

Useful websites
St Andrews and Edinburgh Diocese
http://www.archdiocese-edinburgh.com/files/pastoral/reconciliation.pdf
Lancaster Diocese
http://www.lancasterdiocese.org.uk/Group/Group.aspx?ID=187686

Church documents
Dives in Misericordia (Rich in Mercy) Pope John Paul II, 1980, www.vatican.va
Reconciliation and Penance, Pope John Paul II, 1984, www.vatican.va
Paenitentiam Agere (Doing Penance), Pope John XXIII, 1962, www.vatican.va

You may find also useful
Anchoring you in Happiness (www.anchoryourfaith.com) Dominican Sisters of St. Joseph/Maryvale Institute) - In 6 sessions of 90 minutes each, Anchoring you in Happiness presents the essential truths of the Catholic Faith. It gives a step by step explanation of the Sacrament of Reconciliation, including an examination of conscience.

Fr Allen Morris, Rector of the Parish of Our Lady's, St John's Wood has produced 'refresher' cards for the sacrament of reconciliation. Perhaps your parish would be interested in contacting Fr Allen for copies?

Notes